FACTORS INFLUENCE ORGANIZATIONAL SUCCESS

JOHN LOK

Contents

Foreword

Introduction

Can any one be one successful CEO? If it is not, what are the unique personal characteristics between one general CEO and one successful CEO ? Instead of personal characteristics, which kinds of skills to any successful CEOs, they will need? Why do some CEOs encounter fail to manage themselves companies? Why do some CEOs feel difficulties to manage themselves companies? This book can indicate some evidences to explain what factors can influence the person can be successful CEO to let readers to understand. Readers can learn whether what personal factors can help general CEO to become excellent CEO in any organizations.

Prologue

Table of content

1

The different characteristics between common CEO and successful CEO

The characteristics of common CEO

What are the common characteristics to general CEO? IN general, CEO person specification includes: High level of self-motivation, creativeness high level of self confidence. So, In general, qualitiies and traits of a chief executive officer, he /she may have courage, passion , but an excellent CEO is draw to change and effective action. Also CEO needs have resillence and drive ability. It means theat the CEOs, leaders ought know that taking risks and making large-scale changes can lead to organizational growth or can fall dramatically.

A CEO must posses certain traits to be an effective leader, e.g. ability to learn from the past experience, strong communication skills, buildinh relationship, realistic optimism, easily understanding, listening people and adapting to necessary managment styles.

What makes a good CEO leader? At a leader, a common CEO needs to posses strong communication skills. From motivating your employees to meeting set deadlines. You should have the ability to communicate your needs, when you hope to become a common CEO. If you want to be a good CEO, you must be consistently clear in your communication. But, some succesful executives may have these 7 perdsonality traits, such as visioning, in-depth problem solving and analysis, attapting change, driving for results, influencing and persuading, managing others, organizational resources allocation.

Hence, it seems that it is not all people these 7 successful Ceo. In fact, many companies own common CEOs more than successful CEOs in human resource view. In general, an organizational leader (CEO) , he /she does not need special management train, he /she depends on his/her past working experiences training to climb up to become the company's leader. SO, taking risks and acceptance fail or acceptance attempt, they may be general CEO personal characteristics . All of these personal characteristics, it is not difficult to own to general CEOs in any organizations. But if the organization hopes to help the business owner to manage himslef/herself overall organizational different departmental operation more effectively and efficiently. The CEO must own unique personal characteristics and excellent managing ability in order to gelp his/her boss to manage whole organization excellently. Hence, one successful CEO must own unique personal skills or abilities and personal judgement characteristics to compare common or general CEOs in any organizations.

For example, when one organization has serios financial

resource allocation to provide different departments challenges, it is the best chance to examine the CEO how to apply shortage financial resource to provide to different departments in order to still keep efficient operation aim. If the CEO can know how to arrange shortage financial resource to provide to salespeople salaries expenditure , shop or office rent, water , electricitiy , telephone fee etc operational expenditure, factory workers salaries and factory machines productive energy expenditure, product manufacturing processing material expenditure etc. resource managment expenditure allocation effectively. Consequently, the overall organizational performance can still keep positive growth, or profit can still raise. Then, I believe that this organization leader may be one successful CEO , he/she does not ne one common CEO or failure CEO role to this organization.

The characteristics of successful CEO

What factors cause the CEO can be one successful leader to his/her organization? What are this CEO personal unique characteristics own? I believe that any successful CEOs must oen unique personal characteristics that common CEOs must not own, I shall explain as below:

Usually , any successful CEO must need time from common CEO to become. Every successful CEO must communicate with their employees using concise, easy-to-understand language, open-mindedness, approachability, growth mindset, ethics, decisiveness. All these characteristics may need to any successful CEO. A chief executive officer (CEO) is the highest-ranking executive in a company , whose primary responsibilities include: making major corporate decisions, managing the overall operations and resources of a company, acting as the main point of communication between the board of directors (the board) and these corporate .

Hence, a successful CEO needs have these 5 key managerial skills: Technical skills, conceptional skills, interpersonal and communication skills, decision-making skills. The roles that a manager plays in the organization require having some skills. Hence, one successful CEO must need to know how to supervise and manage stsffs for his / her overall organization. A successful CEO also needs to understand every part and function of the business: accounting, finance, HR, marketing , legal , operation supply chain, sales and information technology. Also, one successful CEO also needs to consider organizational cultural fit, industry understanding , building good soft communication skills between staffs and him/her or between customers and its sale service staffs. Moreover, a successful leader with a CEO mindset has a clear direction for the future, and is not afraid to share it. Do not be scared to set yourself, when you are the organizational CEO and your team, ambitious and exciting goals, sure that you have smaller, achieveable steps in these as well. So you can maintain motivation.

For next example, if you are your firm's CEO, you can help your firm shareholders grew in power and their demand for booming stock prices led to booming pay. It means that you 's CEO salaries increase or decrease, it depends on share price driven salaries, when your organization's share price can often keep high price position to compare similar competitors ' share prices. Then, you 's CEO salary may keep increase, because your can manage firm's share price often keeps on high price position in share market. However, one successful CEO must need to own there managerial skills in order to help his/her organization can grow rapidly. The managerial skills may include as below:

Technical skill, it means that the abilities, knowledge, or expertise required to perform specific, job-related tasks. Technical skills are related to jobs in science, engineering, technological, manufacturing or finance. They are learnt through on-the-job experience or structured learning, e.g. data analysis, project management, technical writing, software proficiency, programming languages, artificial intelligence, machine learning, data engineering, visualization, network and information security, cloud computing.

The next is conceptual skill, a successful CEO also needs have conceptual skill, it is the ability to analyze and evaluate whether a company is achieving its goals and its business plan. Conceptual skills are skills that enable individuals to identify , conceptualize and solve problems. It is important in the workplace because it allows professionals to think and woth though abstract ideas and come up with multiple solutions to complex issues. Hence, conceptual skills include the ability to view the organization as a whole, understand how the various parts are interdepentend, and assess how the organization relates to its external environment. These skills allow managers to evaluate situations and develop alternative courses of actions. Conceptual skills may include: abstract thinking, analytical skills, congnitive skills, communication, contextualizinf, creative thinking, critical thinking, decision making. Hence, one successful CEO may be a conceptual person, who is one conceptual thinker, he /she has an understanding of why something is being done. The conceptual thinker can think at an abstract level and easily applythe CEO himself/herself insights to the suitation. So, any comon CEO may attempt to improve conceptual thought processing and increase work performance by these methods:

Observe leadership. using challenges as case studies, seeking outside knowledge, staying up-to-date on the industry, applying new practices, disucssing concepts with colleagues, finding a mentor, learning about the organization. So, one successful CEO needs to own critical thingking skills: Analysis, interpretation, inference, explanation, self-regulation, open-mindedness and problem solving, strategic thinking includes careful and deliberate anticipation of threats to guard against and opportunities to pursue.

Ultimately strategic thinking and analysis can help CEO to lead to a cleear set of goals, plans, and new ideas have abstract thinking and feeling, it is the ability to understand concepts that are real, such as freedom. So, analytical skills refer to the ability to collect and analyze information , problem solve and make decisions. Successful CEO can know how to use analytical skils when detecting patterns, brainstorming, observing , interpreting data and making decisions based on the multiple tailors and options available to you, such as the organizational CEO, e.g. creative thinking visual art, communication skills and open-mindedness to any one successful CEO, he /she ought own.

Finally, successful CEO needs have excellent interpersonal communication and decision making skill. Why is decision making and communication an important skill? It can help any CEo to raise the ability to make a decision of good leadership skills. Decision making is an on-going process in every organization, large or small. Having critical thinking skills allow the CEO to ascertain the problem and come up with a solution that is benefical to the company and its employees. So, one successful CEO needs to own soft and hard skils both.

For making decision for the organization, the successful CEO must have decision making skill to find the best solution to the challenge in process. He /she can define the problem, challenge or opportunity clearly, generate of possible solutions or responses, evaluates the costs and benefits or pros and associated with each option, selects a solution or response and knows how to implement the option chosen clearly.

Any CEO can learn how to improve decision making in workplace, such as following these steps: starting with the desired outcome, or goals, rely on data and insights to spot patterns, use S.W.O.T analysis, simulate the outcomes, trust your instincts and identify your cognitive biases. Identifying critical factors which will affect the outcome of a decision, evaluate options accurately and establish priorities, anticipate outcomes and see logical consequences, navigate risk and uncertainty,, reason well in requiring quantitative analysis. On conclusion any one CEO must need time to improve his/her hard and soft skills in order to become one successful CEO to his /her organization.

2

What skills to one successful CEO owns

We can learn that it is difference between one common CEO and unique successful CEO personal characteristics. Then, it beings this question: What are the skills that one successful CEO ought own? I believe that one successful CEO ought own these skills that one common CEO he /she won't own.

Building excellent communication skill:

Top performing CEO, ough know that strong communication skills are the secret to influence final success. Successful CEOs understand that influence is required if they are to inspire people to willingly act upon what they have to say. Highly influential CEOs deliver on these communication skills daily as below:

Successful CEOs understand the importance of clear, concise communication. They recognize that in the absence of simplicity comes confusion. For example, one organizational CEO sent an email to his employees listing only three objectives he wished for the company to focus on : " customers, team and execution". Instead of providing a dozen areas of opportunity . This CEO also maintained a short list of objectives that were clear. He kept employee goals concise, guiding them to focus to perform excellent services to let customers feel satisfactory. Such as this case, it explains that where one CEO focuses on concise and clear communication, he makes it easier for others to follow. This level of influence ensures that others remember what was said and are inspired to act accordingly.

Top CEOs are known for their sharp minds, and business acumen. They know that frequent communication between employees and senior leadership to be very important in their ability to stay engaged. For conference discussion case, when a successful CEo discusses ongoing company objectives and action items. he begins each all by sharing status updates of previous discussions, including what the executive staff is doing to secure the company's future. Each call concludes with a 30 minute open question forum, where all empllyees have the chance to ask questions and on ideas the executives discussed. Allowing employees to collaborate and share ideas creates a sense of ownership . It permits insight into the company's goals and encourage employees to engage in its success with ideas of their own.

By creating an atmosphere, successful CEOs encourage employees to share ideas. As a result, CEOs build stronger relationships and deepen trust in leadership . For example, when one CEO maintains an open-door policy and is known for frequently visiting employees on the floor, no matter the department or position. As a result, the CEO builds personal relationships that foster trust and candidacy that only comes with real influence. So , the difference between the successful CEO's communication skill and common CEO's communication skill is that a common CEO has influence based solely on his /her title may intimidate employees to act on direction, but successful CEO is a leader who influences others to act willingly has establish the trust and credibility necessary for lasting success. Unfortunately, too may ledaers fail to share this level of detail with their staffs leading employees to question their intention. They neglect communication weaknesses that need improvement . As a result, the entire organization will benefit from improved performance and communication . When leaders admit they are not perfect and are willing to improve, employees follow suit.

What makes a CEO successful? Findings from a database of 17,000 c-suite assessments reveal that successful CEOs demonstrate four specific behaviors that prove critical to their performance. They are decisive, they engage for impact, they adapt proactively, and they delive reliably. So, as a leader, you need to posses strong communication skills. From motivating your employees to meeting set deadlines, you should have the ability to communicate your needs and even show your employees how things are down. If you want to be a good CEO, you must be consistently clear in your communication.

What is the most important skill to a CEO? In short, the single important role of a CEO is to make absolutely certain that the right CEO is running the company and then do what is necessary to encourage that CEO's effectiveness, strategy, vision, culture shareholder value, all crucial and all within the scopr of the CEO's role. Hence, successful CEO needs to know whether what he/ she actually does. A chief executive officer (CEO) is the highest ranking executive in a company, whose primary responsibilities include making major corporate decisions, managing the overall operations and resources of a company, acting as the main point of communication between the board of directors. Hence,

CEO needs to report to the board of directors, with most CEOs being members and sometimes chair of the board, president, they report to the CEO and the board of directors and cometimes they are board members.

Hence, a CEO needs to understand every part and function of the business: accounting, finance, HR, marketing, legal , operations, supply chain , sales , information technology . In business speak, the CEO's job is to define the mission (purpose), strategy (direction), and metric (pace and performance). These three elements provide the essential elements that a growing company needs to be able to perform. So, a successful CEO must need to find the effective strategy to help his/her company to solve any challenges in ay time. When the chairman technically has higher level power, the CEO is indeed the boss of a company. The CEO does by the law answer to their board of directors, which is ultimately headed by the chairman. In general., the CEO job starts when the organization reaches about 20 employees, prior to 20 employees, the job resembles more of a product management role. CEOs at this stage are trying to develop a visable product and generate some revenue.

In general, successful chief executives tend to demonstrate four specific behaviors that prove critical to their performance. For example, holding people accountable and the ability to motivate a team, high-performing (CEO) do not necessarily stand our for making great decisions all the time, rather they stand our for being more decisive. They make decisions earlier, faster, and with greater conviction. Also, they do so consistently, even with incomplete information, and in unfamiliar domains . Interestingly, the highest IQ executives , they are intellectual complexity, when the quality of their decisions is often good, because of their pursuit of the perfect answer, they can take tool ong to make choices or set clear priorities and their teams pay a high price. These smart but slow decision makers, their teams either grow frustrated , which can lead to the attrition of valuable talent ot become overcautious themselves.

Moreover, high-performing CEOs understand that a wrong decision is often better than no decision at all. It means that a bad decision was better than a lack of direction. Most decisions can be undone, but a successful CEO has learnt to move with the right amount of speed. To that end, successful CEOs also knows when not to decide, whether a decision should actually be more lower down in the organization and if delaying, it is a week or a month time, would allow important information without causing harm. Hence, strong performers balance keen insight into their stakeholders' priorities with focus on delivering business results. They start by developing an understand of their stakeholders' needs and motivations and get many people on board by driving for performance. So, CEO needs to bring others along plan and execute disciplined communications and influencing strategies. Indeed, the skilled CEO gains the support of their colleagues by confidence that they will lead the team to sucess, even if that means taking uncomfortable or unpopular moves. These CEOs do not shy away from conflict in the pursuit of business goals. The ability to handle different viewpoints significantly faster than average.

Factors Influence CEO Success Or Fail

In fact, any CEOs will be influenced to succeed or how how to manage their organizations by personal psychology and personal skills or knowledge and external environment factors. However, CEO is such leader role to any organizations. Can owning high level leadership skillful

CEOs manage their organizations more eaily to compare owning low level leadership skillful CEOs? May leadership skill be main factor to influence any one CEO's person success or fail? I shall attempt to explain as below?

In fact, I feel any CEo must need have these kinds of leadership skills. They ma y include: First, recognizing strengths, everybody with an organization has their strengths, and it is essential that you are able to identify the strengths of individuals, and recognizing weaknesses, second, reacting to employee needs, third, clarity and fourth, willingness to make tough decisions and conflict managment skill. Why does every CEO need have leadership skill? Effective leaders have the ability to communicate well, motivate their team, handle and delegate responsibilities, listen to feedback and have the flexibility to solve problems in an ever changing workplace. Hence , in CEO personal psychological view, an excellent CEO is drawn to change and effective action, courage , passion and resilence and drive attitude . A good leader knows that taking risks and making large-sacle changes can lead to organizational growth or can fall dramatically.

Why is CEO leadership important to the performance of a firm? Research evidence provides overall support for the positive relationship between leadership and firm performance (Lowe et al, 1996). CEOs with transactional leadership can successfully manage goal accomplishment and contribute to the enhancement of the firm performance. So, it seems that CEO's leadership has indirect or direct relationship to inflience his / her whole organizational performance whether it can grow up rapidly or slowly, even fall fown rapidly or slowly, because if the firm's CEO can not manage different department teams cooperate efficiently. Then, the firm's leader personal leadership effort may influence whole organization different department teams to cooperate smoothly. Although, CEO must not need to contact all department staffs every day, but he /she needs to contact any department managers in order to know whether their departments have any challenges , when managers feel difficulties to solve. If the CEO had low level leadership ability, he /she won't discuss with any department managers to conclude the best opinions to solve the challenges more easily. For example, when financial budget department manager discovered that his organization had deficit challenge recently. If he can not solve lack of cash available problem. Then, his organization's deficit will be increased easily. Consequently, it will influence staffs salaries can not pay on time, it won' t have cash to buy enough manufacturing material to prepare to be supplied to manufacture to provide products to provide to market to sell, factory can not have enough money to buy new productive machines to replace old productive machines etc. different kinds of organizational operational needs.

However, if the CEO owning high level leadership skills, he may know hoe to lead this financial budget manager to solve " deficit" challenge. Although, deficit seems to be simple matter, but if this financial budget manager can not know how to manage cash available in order to allocate to different departments operations, e.g. allocating the limiting amount of cash to urgent departments to use in prior. Then, deficit challenge will increase cash shortage number more seriously. So, high leadership skill mist need to any one organizational CEO in order to help his/her organization can solve any challenges more efficiently and easily. Otherwise, low leadership effort owning CEO only influences his/her organization can not grow up more rapidly, even it can fall down rapidly. Consequently, the organization will only liquidate or it will be sold out rapidly. What does excellent leadership skill need to CEO? Many psychologists indicate excellent leadership may include these essential elements: Integrity, ability to delegate, communication, self - awareness, gratitude, learning agility, influence effort, empathy.In common, characteristics of a good leader, he / she can help staffs and makes the essential large-sacle decisions that keep the organization can operate efficiently and reduce challenges occur. Integrity is especially important for top-level executives who are charting the organization's actions and making countless other significant decisions. Ability to delegate , delegating is one of the core responsibilities of a leader, the goal enables the CEO's direct reports, facilitate teamwork, provide autonomy, lead to better decision making and help the CEO's direct reports grow. Effective leadership and effective communication are intertwined.

So, any CEOs need to be able to communicate in a variety of ways, from transmitting information to coaching your staffs (managers). Any CEO must be able to listen to , and communicate with, a wide range of staffs across roles, social identities and more. The quality and effectiveness of communication across the CEO's organization directly affect trhe success of the CEO's business strategy. So, better communication skill can actually improve the CEO's organizational culture. Self-awareness is focuses skills for leadership. The better leadership skill to the CEO , he / she can understand himself / herself managing ability, the more effective , he /she can do. Do you know how other people view you or how you show up at work?

Gratitude can lead to higher self-esteem, reduced depression and anxiety, learning agility is the ability to

know what to do when you do not know what to do. So, great leaders are great learners, with strong learning agility to get started , when you are one organization's CEO in beginning, you must need to learn how to influence your whole organizational staffs behaviors to be the perfect.
" Influence" may be through locial , emotional or cooperative appeals, is a component of being an effective leader, influence is quite different from manipulation, and it needs to be done and it requires emotional intelligence and trust. Empathy is correlated with job performance and is a critical part of emotional intelligence and leadership effectiveness. A successful leadership CEO needs have empathetic behaviors towards his / her direct reports, empathy can be for improving workplace conditions. Courage is such that when the CEO wants to voice a new idea, provides feedback to a direct report or flag a concern for someone above him / her. That is part of the reason courage is a key skill for good leaders. Rather than avoiding problems or allowing conflicts to faster, courage enables leaders to step up and move things in the direct direction. A workplace with high levels of psychological safety and a strong coaching culture will further support truth and courage. Finally CEO needs to know how to treat people with respect on a daily basis is one of the most important things . A leader can do that it will ease tensions and conflict, create trust, and improve effectiveness.
On conclusion, when the CEO can know how to build these psychological and emotion feeling, then the CEO can be trained to improve leadership skill in order to know hoew to manage his / her organization efficiently and effectively.

Can training provision raise CEO leadership

Any organizational CEO is the top level managerial position. So, it is one job to anyone. Any organizational positions may have training provision in order to improve the staff personal job skills, e.g. organizations can provide internal accounting training to accounting clerk, even accounting manager training in order to let they can learn company's accounting policy in order to improve their accounting tasks more proficient, or a law firm can provide legal draft training to general law clerks in order to improve their legal draft writing skils, or one company's data processing department can provide data processing training to improve data processor typing speed to learn more proficient to type its documents, or property agent firm can provide property sale speaking training to its property sale agents to improve their property sales presentation skill or insurance agent firms can provide insurance sale speaking training to its insurance sale agents to improve their insurance sales skills.

Hence, it seems that any organizational positions may apply training methods to improve any staff individual performance in any organizations. So, it brings this question: Can organizations provide training to improve CEO performance to achieve more proficient? To answer this question, we need to suppose same kinds of business CEO positions , they ought be trained to improve their performance. If it is true, whether what kinds of businesses CEO positions, they may be applied training method to improve their managerial skills? How and why to these kinds of business CEO positions, they can be trained to improve their proficiency? I shall attempt to answer as below:

In fact, general CEO typically have a bachelor's or master's degree in business administration or a fiels related to their industry. Some CEO positions require that candidates have a master's or even depending on the industry , education, for instance. So, one university CEO or president, he /she needs have education psychology master or doctorate level to any kinds of degree. They need have high educational level to do university leader. Hence, CEO, training can focus on learning or educational aspect, e.g. certified CEO program is general education certification course designed for business leaders globally (CEO senior managers) and aspiring business leaders who are looking to build upon existing qualifications and business experience.

What does CEO coach training method mean?

However, every CEO needs a coach in organization , because a coach suports the CEO to manage conflict effectively often decisoin of the CEO please one group and displease another. The CEO needs a partner who the CEO can be open with, one who is going to be sensitive, and objective, honest and respectful. Hence in any organizations, a coash can teach the CEO these managing skills to manage their organizations more easily, e.g. flexibility, value driven decision making, delegating, leadership, clear vision implementation.

Hence, in general, coach training needs ususally take 2 to 3 years to complete. The organizational CEO will does on the-job-training and spend time with a training provider. Employers will set their own entry requirements. So, in popular, many CEOs use a CEO coach over the course of their career. No athlete would be embarrassed they use a coach. Yet, CEOs believe they do not need a coach of their own. However, any organization is the final deicion making person, when the organization feels that the CEO's managerial effort is poor, it can attempt to provide a proficient managing experience coach to train this CEO's management skill in order to achieve this organization's CEO ability requirement within 2 to 3 years. For example, a CEO peer group training, interchangably called CEO peer groups or networks, these organizations generally arrange reqular meetings in confidential environments where CEOs can share ideas, best practices, experiences and advice together to attempt how to improve their managerial skills. So, executives look for in a coach, a good executive coach does not need to have the exact background or experience as the CEO , but a familiarity will help him or her better understand the CEO thinking and needs. More importantly, the CEO coach needs skills, the CEO either does not have and wants to attain, or ones that can help strength the CEO opportunity areas.

In general, what leaders want from coaching. Coaching empowers leaders to do expectional work. Coaches establish and advantageous relationship that uncovers hidden strengths and weaknesses within the leader. Goals will be created to enable leaders to indicate their weaknesses and track their progress. What is better up coaching? Coaching training can address the CEO must pervasive organizational challenges with the organizational unique combination of coaching to achieve a growth approach to mental fitness and organizational health more effectively.

Have a CEO coach is similar to the executive or leadership coach , but with the added responsibility of working with the CEO who is working in the firm. So, coach can attempt to help the CEO potentially make the most significant difference in the company's success and lives and careers of those who work for the company. Hence, any organizations can provide executive or leadership coach to improve the CEO's leadership skills by these 5 caoching styles, such as below:

Democratic coaching, this method gives the term freedom

and accountability, with the coach stepping in only when meeded to keep the process going, or authoritarian coaching, holistic coaching, authcratic coaching and vision coaching training methods, for example, entrepreneur coach can help new and existing business owners with any number of tacks to foster their entrepreneurship. In fact, entrepreneurship is not about having a business, but about having an entrepreneurship mind. So, CEOs can be trained from any style of coach in order to improve their management and leadership skills to more proficient in their organizations. So, it means that coaching training is one kind of effective training method to improve CEO's performance in any organizations.

On conclusion, I believe that it is only one kind of training method to train any organizational CEOs to become proficient CEO, it is coaching training method, instead of providing general educational level to the CEO for leadership knowledge, because coach training is one kind of organizational leadership practice training, it can satisfy any CEOs to raise leadership effort effectively to help the CEO to manage his/her organization easily.

3

New Business Foundation Strategies

Any new business founders, they ought hope their new businesses can run long time. The question concerns that how they can help their new businesses run long time, e.g. at least above 5 years . I shall attempt to apply behavioral economic theory to solve this common challenge as below.

Keeping a new business is in difficult economic time is challenging. Every new business is different and each carries its own risks and rewards in behavioral economy view. These sifferences cause some new business founders attempt to copy another similar new business founder strategy. Still, these are save general strategies business owners can follow to help themselves new businesses to copy another similar new business strategy succeeds in possible.

However, some of these copying another new business founder strategy's owner still feels their sopying another new business founder strategy may help them to succeed. So, they still have risk or they may encounter failure, if the another similar new business founder strategy can not be suitable to be adopted to themselves new business similiarly. So, it explains that why some new business founder can not keep their new businesses can run long time, because they feel the other similar new business founders their strategies can help to develop their new businesses succeed together. But in fact, there are may new business founders their copying strategy decisions are wrong. They feel their copying another new business founder's strategy can help them to develop in success. So, their new business strategies ought also help their new businesses to develop or grow long time. However, there are many new businesses can not run above 5 years, due to there new business founders choose the wrong copying strategies from another similar new business or old business competitors.

New business founder needs to look at the big picture, it means that long term customer behavior change picture. Because consumer behaviors must often change suddenly in any time. So, any new business founder ought attempt to discover whether what their product buyers behaviors will change after 5 years, even 10 years in predicting. People have a tendency to attack the most obvious immediate prodblems without hesitation. That's understandable and might make good business sense in some suitations. However, it is also advisable to step back and look at the big picture to see what is still working and what might need changing.

Its an opportunity to better comprehend the size and the scope of exciting problem and further understand your new firm's decision model, determining how its strengths and weaknesses come into play. What is a business model? The term business model refers to a firm's plan making a profit. It identified target market, e.g. which is age customer group, where is the geographical sale place, and anticipated expenses. However, business models are improtant for both new and established businesses. They help new developing companies attract investment, recruit talent, and motivate management and staff. Establishing businesses should reguarly update their business plans or they will fail to anticipate trends and channelgens. So, business models both levers are pricing and costs. It is a high -level plan for profitably , a business in a specific marketplace. A primary component of the business model is the value proposition. This is a description of the goods or services that a new business offers and why they are desirable to customers, ideally stated in a may that differentiates the products or services from its competitors.

A new business enterprise's business model should also cover projected startup costs and financing sources, the target customer base for the new business, marketing strat egy , a review of the competition, and projections of revenue ans expenses. It may also define opportunities in which the new business can partner with other established companies, e.g. the new business model for an advertising business may identify benefits from an arrangement for referrals to and from a printing company. So, successful new businesses need have good business models that allow them to fulfill client needs at a competitive price and a sustainable cost. Over time, many new businesses revise their business models from time to time to reflect changing business environments and market demands. However, the business model may not tell new business founder everything about a company's prospects, but the investor who underatands the business model can make better sense of the financial data.

New business founder also needs to consider

organizational internal matter, e.g. suppose a new business founder discovers that two employees are making mistakes with inventory that cause certain supplies to be overstocked or understocked. When a initial reaction might be to fine those employees. It might be wiser to examine whether the manager who hires and supervises them properly trained time. If the manager is to blame, that person could be fired, but this might not be the best solution. If the manager's relationship with client have a history of bringing in repeat business and substantial revenue. They are likely someone, you would want to keep. However, retraining might be a better alternative than termination.

Infact, by thoroughly reviewing the strengths and weaknesses of the employees, the owner is looking at the issue from a top-down perspective, reducing or eliminating the chance that the problem will occur when avoiding a change that could adversely impact future sales. Hence, a similar kind on analysing how youe new products or services fit into the marketplace in your new business beginning stage, how the economic crisis has affected your customers and suppliers and all the other key aspects of your new business. You need to know how well your new business model fits the current environment and forecast what various alternative scenarios of the future mighr mean for it.

For one interesting new business behavioral economic view to recuriting new employees view example, any new business owners or large corporational founders tend to be either wise or follish when they hire the least expensive workers sometimes, the productivitiy of these workers may be suspect. Hiring one worker who costs 20% more than the average workers, but works 40% more effectively make of crisis. By seeking resumes and interviews from new applicants. New business founders can make change to new staff when needed to increase efficiency. So, how to choose any department new staff recruitment , it is very important to influence the new business furher develops for long time. Don't sacrifice quickly, keeping a handle on costs is crucial in tough times. Owners need to stay on the offensive and get employees on board with changes that are being made. However, any one new business founders need have good sense to predict when their new products or new services need to be changed in order to adopt customer behavioral changing environment.

ON conclusion, so any new business founders hipe to keep themselves new businesses can run long time, they must need to know " consumer behavioral psychology" how and why to cause their change in order to implement the most effective new business strategy to improve their sale methods to achieve the most satisfactory level to their potential clients' purchase needs or service needs in long time. Consequently , their new businesses ought keep long running time in this old and new product / service competitor market.

Avoiding new business low value method

Internet marketing promotion strategy

Any new business founders do not hope their new business market worth falls rapidly or share price falls rapidly. What facors may cause new business share price or market value falls rapidly? What methods to help new businesses keep the same share price is stable long time or market value can be kept in the stable worth, even share price can be influenced the rise or market value can be influenced to rise? I shall attempt to explain some useful methods, they may influence new business market value to avoid falls down, or share price can rise more easily.

TO avoid new business low value, these ways may be used in developing new business. They may include: Knowing what your client individual actual need, e.g. rice cooker product, cooking rice function must need , but avoiding to spend long time or short time to cook rice rapidly, big rice cooker size to cook more rice, long time keeping rice warm function. All these factors may influence rice cook buyers individual choices. Some housewives also need the kind of rice cooker has above all these functions, before they make rice cooker purchase decision. So, knowing what your clients real needs, they are essential to product manufacturers, offering great customer service, e.g. repair sevice, after sale enquiry (following up equiry to the client, nurture existing customers and look for new sale need opportunities, use social media attending networking events, give back to your community, measure what works and refine your approach as you go. So, if the business founder can manage sale and customer, service both teams to achieve the best service performance to let clients feel , then they may persuade many clients continue choose to continue to buy their products more easily. So, salespeople and customer service staffs training method may be one main influential factor to help the organization to raise market share value. If the organization can design useful training course to raise its salespeople sale skills or customer service staff service performance.

Which businesses can be started with less investment? For India country example, these low investment business wil be helped the new business founder to earn the most profitable, e.g. dropshipping is one of the most successful business in India, because in India, even global there are many tall offices need dropshipping equipment to transport window cleaners to clean tall office windows. So, dropshipping cleaners'window ability may influence India deopshipping firm share price changes to rise up or fall down. Because India dropshiping companies window clean workers window cleaning performance can bring property management company clients to make dropshipping window cleaning service provider choice.

I mean that India dropshipping office window or global dropshipping office windoe clean service providers, their new business market value or high stable shar e price value, their value is depended on whether their dropshipping window cleaners clearning window skills or window clean priperty management clients' window clean needs. So, for dropshipping office cleaning service provider case example, how to improve dropshipping office window cleaning workers' windows clean ability, it is only one influential method to influence dropshipping office window cleaning firm service providers their shares prices whether they can keep stable market position, even share price can be risen easily. How to improve dropshipping office cleaning workers' office windows cleaning skill is very important to influence dropshipping office window service providers' shares prices are at the stable high price level. For courier company example, how to improve courier service performance, e.g. shorten the document / goods delivery time between the document or goods sender countey and the document or goods country receiver, when the document or goods can not bt delayed to send to the overseas receiver whose home from the another country sender, e.g. From US sends the document to China in common general couriers need 5 days , but the US courier company can send the documents to China, it only needs 2 days delivery time. Then, it may attract many China goods or documents receiving clients to choose the US courier service providers. So, how to keep the US new courier servier providers, or market value or share price value, it depends on whether it may help its overseas documents or goods receiving clients to reduce how long time to let they can receive the documents or goods from US. So, the avoiding delivery time delay is the import factor to influence courier goods / documents delivery service provider new business market value.

Moreover, any one new business founder may promote themselves new business in a low budger. These methods may include: posting amazing content on your new firm's blog, creating a google my new business account, building a free or cheap email list, contributing an article to an industry magazine, attending local networking events, co-sponsor a contest. So, internet channel may help any new business to build a rapid promotion network to let many people to know that this kind of new business exist, it aims to let potential clients number increases in short time in possible. So, internet may be a kind of new promotion tool to help any new business market share value rises in short time, the internet strategies for effective promotion of new business, e.g. creating a website, geting listed on google, advertise on facebook, email customers, and potential customers use google Adwords, paid media advertising , social networks and viral marketing, internet marketing, email marketing, direct selling, point-of-purchase marketing, co-branding, cause marketing , conversational marketing .

All of these internet promotion methods may help new businesses to rise market growth value or share price in short time. Hence, internet promotion method is preferable to choose to compare general TV, advertising , newspaper, advertising, magazine advertising, radio adverting, sales promotion, general selling, publicity promotion methods because internet promotion marketing is one kind method, it may bring the new product or new service providing message to let many potential clients to know from the new firm's email ot website in short time rapidly. It is one kind of new global promotion method for any kinds of new busienss development in beginnning.

So, any new business founder may prefer to choose internet promotion method in orde to let many potential cients to know their new products ot services are existence. So, attracting new customers method may use social media optimizing the new business founder's social media account, improves website and engage with loyal customers, give branded gifts , referral discounts, social media contects, and giveways, sending email to survey customers, researching your competitors and finding out who their customers are, target email advertisement, smart social media, responding to every email, tweet , facebook comment, e-publish user reviews from internet media channel. All of these new internet promotion strategies may help any kinds of new businesses to promote their products or services to let clients to know in short time rapidly from internet media promotion channel. The internet promotion marketing strategy is one kind of low cost promotion strategy, low cost marketing stragtegy for startups, cheapest new businesses to start and focused low cost strategy company.

Why internet promoting strategy can help new business to avoid low market value? The reason is simple, because when the new firm sends one email message to let any one country's email user to know. This new product or new service email message can let global any one emaill user to know that this new product or new service business is existence in market. When the email user receives the new business' semail message, it may keep in itself email box. So, the email user won't lose the one email message and it can often remember this new product, or new service provider is existence in market. So, any one email user when he/ she receives new product or service provider 's email, this email is such as the private advertisment between the new business founder and the email receiver. So, email advertising is different general product magazine, TV, newspaper , radio advertisment. It is public promotion advertisement.

Hence, the feeling of private advertisment, it is the most influential factor to persuade potential consumers to choose to buy the new product or use the new service from this provider, because when the potiential client receives the email promotion from the new product/ new service provider, he /she may feel surpise to raise interest to click the advertismeent email to see whether what benefits can be given ti him/her if he /she chooses to buy the new product or use the new service. If one say, the new product / new service provider can send about 1,000 promotion email to let global 1,000 different countries possible potential clients to know its new product/new service is existence in market. Consequently, this email network promotion method can help this new business founder to advertise his / her new product /new service to let global 1,000 email users to know in one day. When, its potential clients number increases, it implies that its new product or new service market existence value will be possible to influence to rise up. Hence, emial promotion method may influence any kinds of new businesses to rise market value in short time in possible, because when may email receivers become to the new business potential clients. Consequently, the new business's share price may be influenced to riase up then its market value may also be follow to influence to rise up. So, it seems that email promotion method may be nowadays a kind of the most effective promotion method to help any new businesses to raise up share price or raise market value in short time.

4

Skills shortages on developing country market

Nowadays , future global job market competition will be trended serious. Any employers will expert their employees own different skills to know how to do their jobs efficiently and effectively and easily. So, future any organization employees ought considerate how to learn different kinds of skills or knowledges in order to prepare to satisfy their future employers‘ different new tasks needs. However, if future any new skillful needs or demands will be raised to future employers' demands. It brings these questions: what skills do global any organization employees need own in general? How to improve or raise employees themselves skills more easily and efficiently? What will happen if future employees do not learn new knowledge to improve or raise themselves skills? Why is learning any new skillful knowledge important ? What will be the possible negative and /or positive consequence if future the organizations do not need their employees to learn any new kinds of skillful knowledge?

Future developing countries need to develop their economy, so they need to employ many employees who own technical skills and /or soft skills. What kind of technical skills and/ or soft skills , the developing countries' employees who will need to order to raise competiton in local job market ? I shall indicate the developing country China example. China is one developing country, employers will need different kinds of skillful labors to assist them to develop their businesses. However, China employers will face skillful labour shortage challenge. Although Chinese young age population is high, but many of them do not to be encouraged to learn enough skillful knowledge to fill future new skillful positions. So, the fast speed of training will be important to influence China supply and demand labour market to be more accurately as well as future China's the quality of labour demand number will be influenced to be raised after they have enough training to learn new skills.

How to solve future China skillful shortage of labour? Firstly, nowadays, China employers need to teach their employees to learn how to use and how to operate robotic skills in China's factories. AI robotic has been early developing, so they need to prepare to learn robotic management and operating technical and soft skills in order to satisfy future China factory automation industry development.

China is one world's factory for low-end products to high quality information products, high end technology and services. So, China will need many high skilled workers to assist manufacturers to manufacture many different kinds of products to export or local sale. Moreover, robotic manufacturing skillful workers will also need because robotic will be accepted to assist manual workers to work in China's any factories. This has led to greater demand for labour wirh upgraded skills and competence. So, it seems that China's orkers need to lern any high technological manufacturing knowledge, e.g. learning how to co-operate with robotics to raise productive efficiencies, which will be future many China's manufacturers' skills need intention.

So, when any one of China manufacturer invests robotics to work in its factory . Then, the China manufacturer's labours ought need to know how to co-operate with th robotics to raise productivities and efficiencies. Moreover, these China service industries, e.g. IT, software, accounting, finance, marketing and customer service management, e.g. waiter, property security, shopping center customer service etc. service occupations. In the future, robotics can also used to participate any one of these service industries' part of tasks in order to raise service performance. So, any one of these service industries' employees need to learn how to operate with robotics in order to achieve the most excellent servvice performances to satisfy consumers' needs. So, China service industries labours ought need to learn how to co-operate or manage service natural robotics to work together more efficiently because future China manufacturers will prefer to employ the labours who know how to co-operate and manage and control any service natural robotics more easily and efficiently in order to achieve the most excellent service performance to satisfy customers needs.

Hence, it seems that China manufacturing and service workers need to spend time and effort to learn how to co-operate with manufacturing natural robotics to manufacture any products in factories efficiently or deliver any cargos in warehouses more efficiently or serve customers to let them to feel excellent service performance in restaurants or shopping centers or properties or offices receiption counters. Then, when their China employers apply robotics to participate to work in factories, restaurants, shopping centers, cinemas, offices or properties reception etc. different working places . These low skillful labours will be dismissed easily, due to robotics can replace them to manufacture any products or provide services to satisfy clients' needs in order to let them to fell robotics' performances are more excellent to compare human service labours or their productive efficiencies are more effort to compare workers. So, future China workers need to learn how to cooperate or manage or contol with robotics to work more efficiently, if they do not expect to be dismissed easily.

Future global skillful labor
soft knowledge skill need

In the future several occupations have been identified as the most frequent movers between all labour market states. The elementary occupations include: waiters, bar staffs, clearners, catering assistants, construction and security service workers, care workers, sales assistants and general clerks etc. So, the low educational level workers can learn these soft wkills to raise whose professional workering level to prepare to do these above positions in global elementary occupation job market.

The changes of employer were most frequent for IT programmers, doctors, electricians, carpenters, skilled workers in global labour market. These skilled occupations will have manpower shortage supply challenge, due to either people feel the educatonal level is under low. So, there has no many people have interest to know these knowledg to prepare their elementary careers. So, these kinds of low skilled occupations will have not enough human power supply to global labour job market also, the high skilled or educational job support.

Moreover, the high skilled occupations also encounter labour shortage issue. The skills in short supply related to experienced candidates e.g. five years or more. For example, pharmaceutical , biogharma and food innovation industries. The occupational shortage roles include: Chemists, analytical scientists, product formulation, analytical development for roles in biopharma, quality control analyst includes pharmaco-vigilance, i.e. drug safety roles. The demand for engineering industry aspect which will aos increase the labour shortage includes process and design (research and development, quality control, automation, lean processes) are skillful labours need to help employers to achieve these intentions. They may include raising competitiveness, boosting productivity and skills availability. So, if future these above any one of occupation labours can not achieve these benefits to satisfy their employers' needs. Then, his/her average weekly or hourly wages will be reduced. It means that the unskilled labour under skilled labour wage can not increased more easily, even they own many year working experiences in any one of above these occupations. If the employer feels the labour is unskilled or below skilled level for any one of these occupations in these any one industry aspect, e.g. wholesale and retal , human health, education, accomodaton and food , construction, professional activities, financial service , public administration, and defence, transportation etc. occupations. Then, these industries' unskilled or below skilled level workers' salaries will be lower level to compare the higher skilled workers who work in any one of these industries.

The reason why future employers need to employ skilled

labours. One explanation for slow recovery in demand in negative impact on investment is a prolonged period of high unemployment. This is led to job weekers left labour market or became unemployable due. So, future low skillful level will be one important factor to cause unemployment in society as well as nowadays labours ought need consider whether their skills are needed to improve in order to avoid future competition in job market.

2.1 Why do future labours need to learn worldwide readiness skills

Future employers need employees own worldwide readiness skills, such as reading , writing and arithmatic. Why do employees need worldwide readiness skills? In the future, high economic growth countries need high wage positions, high opportunity jobs which need a large number of skills required of job candidates of these positions " job readinss" and not " job training" , which support developments of these importance and widely desired skills won't only support the success to high-opportunity positions, but also be developed for future success in the competitive global economy. Because real-time business intelligence is needed for the talent marketplace to employ talent employees. So, it explains that it will have many future employers hope to employ owning readiness skillful employees to help them to develop their businesse intelligently. Hence, present employees ought need to hard to train readiness skills to prepare whose future employers' job requirements in the future competitive global job market.

2.2 Why these occupations need readiness skills

In the future these occupations will need to raise readiness skills. For example, mathematical science, teachers (post-secondary), management analysts, computer and information systems, managers, first-line supervisors of construction traders, solar photovoltaic installers. All of these occupations , employers need staffs to own good readiness analytic ability to help them to do more accurate real-time business intelligent decisions. The representative occupations include oral and written communication skills, project management, teamwork, marketing and creativity . Moreover, they need to own specific technology skill, deep science and math or even most business skills as well as these skills are "soft" skills more than hard skills. These kinds of occupation employees need own cooperative effort, creativity, problem solving, detail orientation and integrity personal characteristics, which are relevant across all knowledge and domains.

Therefore, in the future, science, technology,engineering and mathematics relevant occupations need to own more readniness and analytic skills more than othe kinds of occupations. Because these organizations need those professionals on knowledge acquisition, literacy analysis, synthesis and critical thinking skills that will impact their organizations to bring more critical thinking beneficial team culture. These occupational top skills will include oral and written communication skills, project management skill, team oriented skill, marketing and creativity skills, problem solving skill, detail oriented skill, self-motivated skills, management and analytical skills, coaching skill, business process modeling skills, work independent skill, strong leadership skills, management experience and business requirements gathering. All of these skills which will be future employers who need to employ these kinds employees who own these skills in preference. Also, all of these skills concentrate on soft skills more than hard skills.

It seems that when above occupational applicants who own any one of thes skills, evn more than one skills. Then, he/ she will have more chance to be selected to employ. Also occupation specific skills requirements are more needed to compare cross-functional skills for above of any one occupation. Because the high concentraton of cross-functional skills require " job readiness" and not " job training" for success, e.g. communicaton, integraton and presentation skills, entrepreneurialism and related skills, microsoft office software skills.

Of particular interest is communication, integration and presentation skills. These skills include ability to seek, evaluate and examine information and data create a reasoned position, present findings and make a case for or advocate for position. So, these skills are very important and they can help future applicants who expect to win any kinds of these positions easily. However, the hard skills can help these applicants to be more successful to win any kinds of these positions when they own these hard skills, e.g. microsoft offic, powerpoint, excel , word, microsoft project etc. softwares.

In conclusion, the global economy is dynamic and many of the skills required for positons in the future will need good technologies and work practices to be developed. The number of skills required t be successful in the jobs forecast to be most in demand in the future is growing. So, it explains that why future any one of these occupations which will need soft skills more than hard skills, due to organizations like to employ the employees who own managerial and analytical effort more than hard skills productive effort to assist their organizations to develop more easily.

2.3 Data -analysis skill needs

In the future, most organizations will have a number of jobs that include data analysis. Economists and labor market forecasters predict occupations need data analytical skill will need much. In addition, fast technological development means th types of technologies and applications workers in this field will need to be familiar with data analytical skill rapidly. It seems that data analytical jobs will have new job opportunity to employees with in-demand skills in future global labor market.

Why and how do employers demand for data analysis skills? Data analysis skills mean the ability to gather, analyze and draw practical conclusions from data as well as communicate data findings to others. The occupations include: data analyst, data scientist, statistician, market research analyst, financial analyst,research manager. In business career, many employers expect to employ statisticans, operations researh analysts, market research analysts and marketing specialists to assist their organizations to gather useful data from market in order to analyze and draw practical conclusions and finding the best solutions or methods to win their competitors.

Therefore, these data analysis jobs will have much need. Large size organizations with 500 or more employees were more likely than small or medium size organizations with 25 to 499 employees to plan hired data analysis positons in the future. For example, human source department will use big data to help make strategic decisions. How HR uses big data . HR will use big data for sourcing, recruitment, or selection, identifying causes of turnover and/or employee retention strategies or trends, managing talent and performance. Why organizations do not use big data. It is possible that they lack of knowledg expertise, the majority of organizatons will have data analysis positions within accounting and finance department, human resources department, business and administration department, information technology department, marketing, advertising and sales department, supply chain and operations department, research and development department, customer service department and other departments. So, future data analysis skill will need to used in different organizational departments.

However, publicly and privately owned for-profit organizations were more likely than government organizations to have data analysis positions in the marketing, advertising and sales function. Also, data analysis skills are required to different levels in any organizations , such as entry level, non-management / individual contributor level, mid-level management level, seniot management or executive level. The analyst, research analyst, market research analyst, scientist-based titles include: data scientists , research scientist, scientist, other descriptive titles include researcher, statistician, mathematician and other . So, data analysis positions will have many different skills to be selected to any one data analysis professional. For example, the data analysis professional can select either to learn the ability to interpret and communicate data analysis results skill or to learn how gathering or analyzing data skill. So, data analysis skill is not onlyone skill, it is more than one skill to let any one employee to select to learn.

Why do organizations need data analysis professionals? On workforce planning aspect, organizatons expect to let strategic direction and content of workforce needed for future business objectives easier, analyzing workforce:

supply analysis, demand analsis and gap analysis more earier, developing action plan : recruiting and training plans to deal with gaps more easier, implementing action plan, monitoring, evaluating and revising plan more easier. So, organizations expect the data analysis professionsla can help them to solve these challenges, such as using of advanced technology solutons to integrate disparate planning sources; data availability and format; accessing to and understanding of the organization's data and analytics, developing business case to gain support from senior management and collaboration among HR staff, managers and executive easier. Future industries need data analysis professionals may include manufacturing health care and social assistance, scientific and technical service, finance and insurance, educational services , government agencies, retail trade, transportation and warehousing, construction, utilities, accomodation, and food services, waste management and remediation services, entetainment, and creation, real estate and rental and leasing , repair and maintenance, agriculture, forestry, fishing and hunting, personal and laundry services etc.

In conclusion, data analysis job need explains why future readiness and data analytical skills will be popular needed in globl labour market , due to these both skills are labour shortage and employers will need employees own big data readiness and data analytical both skills in order to win whose competitors more easier.

2.4 What are regional dynamic skills of global labour market demand

Businessmen expect to improve better economic environment, they will prefer to recruit the most sought after skills of intelligent employees to bring positive beneficial impact to organizations. However, technology and digisation has had a significant influence on workers. Future globalization will trend digital economic development. Hence, it will influence workers' skills to be changed also. In fact, not all changes are positive because some workers will possible lose jobs, either due to new technology replaces their jobs or they lack enough effort to improve their skills in global digital economic labour market environment.

It brings this question: What are regional dynamic skills need whn digital busines environment is growing. In fact, organizations will continue to deal with skills shortages, labour markets across the global are continually changing. so, more employers and workers will need to adopt innovate working pattern, e.g. on call jobs, freelance jobs will grow popularly. The greater flexibility afforded to employ regardly.

Finally, digitalisation includes artificial intelligence, big data , online platforms. All these new technology will influence future employees how to worker. For example, they can apply online platform to work at home conveniently. So, they do not need to go to offices. They can finish their jobs and send to their employers by email easily. This kinds of job pattern can raise efficiencies and employers do not need go to offices often.

An important implication of innovating working which needs the employees who own digital skills in order to serve organizations more efficiently. So, employers are increasingly able to access demographics that were hitherto less active in labour markets. For example, future more women are joining the labour market because part time and self employment opportunities make it easier. This kinds of job pattern can raise efficiencies and employees do not need go to offices often.

An important implication of innovating working which needs the employees who own digital skills in order to serve organizations more efficiently. So, employers are increasingly able to access demographic that were hitherto less active in labour markets. For example, future more women are joining the labour market because part time and self employment opportunities make it easier to manage family with work life. So, digital skilling needs will cause many women lose jobs in possible. If the women lack digital job skills. Because high digital skill occupations need, like those requiring research, medical treatment and architectural design occupational digital skills are more common in the services sector, more women who own digital skill who can compete to win.

High digital skill occupations more easier than men because employers usually select female to do high skill occupations easier than make. However, if those professional service female employees can not learn how to apply digital skills to do these researchs medical treatmentm architectural design professional service jobs. Then, it is also different for these professional service femal employees to raise competition in global labour professional service market. So, these professional service female employees need to learn how to apply digital to do themselves jobs in future global professional service labour market. Otherwise, if the male professional service employees can attempt to learn how to apply digital skill to do themselves jobs in order to improve efficiencies and service performance to satisfy patients, such as medical service needs, school search service needs, construction firms‘ building needs. Then, the owning high digital technology skillful female employees will be more easier to find the professional service jobs which need digital skill more easier than the lacking digital skill female service professionals in future global digital service professional labour market.

On the other robotic communication skill need aspect, future employers expect workers to know how to communicate with robots to work efficiently in any working environment if the employers need robotc to serve their organizations. For example, communication between the robots on factory floors, and between people and robots could allow robots to start and stopr processes based on real-time conditions around them and alert people when there is a problem, so robots could increase their own efficiency if the workers could monitor themselves and determine when they needed maintenance; efficiency would also be improved if machines and robots could make production decisions on their own by. For example, ordering new suppliers when existing inputs into a production process run low. The increase in productivity of industrial robots will likely reduce the number of manual jobs on the shop floor.

At the same time, the increased output made possible by such robots will mean that manufacturers need more people in accounting, finance, sales, advertising and other roles. The increase in putput may also drive increased employment on manufacturers' supply chains. Hence, future employers expect to employ the workers who can know how to communicate with robots to work efficiently in order to raise productivity in any working environment. It means that it the worker can know how to control and communicate with the robots to work together in the team. Then, his/her communication and controlling robotic skill will help the organization's team to work efficiently and raise productivity in order to reduce time waste and human waste and resource waste considerately. So, future shortage of communication and controlling robotic skillful workers number will increase. It has much beneficial to workers who choose to attempt to learn how to communicate and control robots to work together in any working environment team efficiently. Because future employers will like to use robots to assist manual workers to attempt to raise productive efficiency in any working environment. So, the need of employees who know how to cooperate or communicate with robots whose talent skills will be useful to any future employers.

Future global business leaders will need human machine cooperation skill. This technological skill includes artificial intelligence (AI and internet of things (IOT), will reshape our working change. These machines will participate to our daily working environment. For instance, many business leaders agree that automated systems will free-up their time as well as they also believe they'll have more job satisfaction by offloading the tasks that they don't want to do to intelligent machines.

Therefore, future leaders will expect humans and machines can work as integrated teams within their organizaton in order to their workforce and machines are already successfully working this way. So, they need to expect future employees can know or learn how to work with automated systems more easily, because many jobs will be participated by automated systems, e..g simple accounting tasks, legal administration tasks etc. clerical tasks. They will be participated with (AI) technology, it learns how to cooperate with (AI) technology to finish simplt clerical tasks efficiently.

Future workers will need have autrmated system

operational skills: They include that how to operate automated systems to free -up workers' time. Workers will need to learn how to operate automated system to better with healthcare tracking devices workers will need to learn how to operate automated systems to absord and manage information in completely different ways. Workers will need to learn how to operate automated systems of smart machines to work as admin. in any orking environments. Workers need be needed to learn how to operate (AI) automated machines to mak more accurate clerical tasks or efficiencies. So, the automated system (robotic) operational skillful workers' demand and number will increase.

In the future, employers need automated machine manufacturing and service with workers cooperation reasons include that clear protocols, will need to be established if autonomous machines fail. So, they need their workers to learn how to control and manage and communicate with autonomous machines skillfully. They believe move they depend upon technology, the more they'll have to lose in the event of a cyber attack. So, skillful workers are real required to let them to know how to cooperate with autonomous machines more efficiently and easily. Computers will need to be able to decipher between good and bad commands, so future employers have much chance to need the owning automated machines operating workers to assist any robots to make more accurate good or bad decision when robots and workers have need to make immediate judgement in their any related job responsibilites aspect.

Therefore, future owning automated machines operating workers' skillful level will be high. It bases on automated machine manufacturing environment trend factor. Finally, future technology will connect the right employee to the high task at the right time. It implies that when future global employers began to accept to apply robots to help them to raise any productivities efficiently. It will influence many manufacturing positions which need to employ any proficient skillful workers who own automated machines operational skills to know how to communicate or manage or control , even supervise any robots to work in teams in any organizational manufacturing environment efficiently. In the future, employers also expect employees to own sufficient digital vision and strategic skills, manifest among other things. They can know how to apply data to demonstrate any senior support and sponsorship digital technological skill. They expect to reduce a skill gap and avoid a lack of employee buying and a workforce culture to change in their digital technologicl manufacturing organizations. Future employers also believe outdated technology that can't work fast enough, data overload, privary and security concerns. So, it explains why it is possible that future employers also need digital working environment and automated robots machines to attempt to achieve raising productive efficient aim.

Moreover, it also explains why digital transformation need will be raised. The reasons include: They feel digital technology can gain employees' buying in , making customer experience a boardroom concern, achieving fair compensation , training and goals and strategy achievement more easily, tasking senior leaders with digital working environment change putting policies and technology to support a fully remote, flexible workforce , empowering lines of team work more efficient, teaching all employees how to code/understanding how to adopt to work with automatic machines or rots in any team efficiently. So, automate machine can raise efficiency in manufacturing society.

In conclusion, in the future business society, employees need to be stronger human machine partnerships. So , future manufacturing or service industries will have digital technology and automated machine robotic technology to assist workers to work in any working environment efficiently. They expect digital technology and automated machine robotic technology anticipation to workers' daily jobs in order to bring positive impacting to the customer experience from business owners to decision makers in marketing, customer service, research and developmnt and finance etc. They also expect technological productivity can bring positive relationship between technology and workers emerging technologies' impact on business and the way workers and automated machine work together.

Future organizational skillful
needs how to influence workforce
change to what kinds of employees

In the future whether in general organizations need what kinds of employees' skills, they expect employee individual own. It is one interesting question. The common skills that employees need to own in order to any duties to any organizational departments efficiently, e.g. human resource, marketing, administrative, logistic etc. different departments. For hospital, school, business, professional occupations etc. different organizations. Whether future school ought implement one system educational method to teach different common skills to students in order to let them to leave schools to jobs more easier.

Future employers need to create new technologies including automation and algorithms, in order to create new high quality jobs and improve the job quality and productivity of the existing work of human employees in any organizations, e.g. accounting department will need intelligence (AI) to assist account clerks to do simple repeating accounting job tasks in order to share their work load and raise performance efficiency or legal organizations will need (AI) to assist law clerks to do simple repeating legal draft or legal document revising job tasks . All future general clerical jobs will apply (AI) technological tools to assist human to job, it will produce a comprehensive platform for managing workforce change.

Hence, human manual(employees) need to learn how to adopt (AI) job participation to assist them to do different kinds of simple clerical jobs in any organizational administrative departments . They , clerical employees or white color workers need to learn how manage or dominate (AI) tool to improve job performance to be better. However, (AI) administrative workforce change, it is not only one kind of job automation change role in any physical offices. It influences future administrative clerks need change a more flexible manner, utilizing remote staffing beyond physical offices and decentralization of operations organizational workforce change.

Instead of (AI) participation to administrative job aspect, (AI) will also participate to manufacturing industry environment aspect, a new human-machine manufacturing workforce change will exist to any factories, warehouses working environment. Scientists predict that in present an average of 71% of total task hours across the industries are performed by humans, compared a 29% by machines. In this average is expected to have shifted to 58% task hours performed by humans and 42% by machines. In fact, nowadays, in terms of total working hours, no work task was yet estimated to be predominantly performed by a machine or an algorithm (AI). But, this

picture is predicted to have somewhat changed with machines and algorithms (AI) on average increasing their contribution to specific tasks by 57% . For example, in the future, 62% of organization's information and data processing and information search and transmission tasks will be performed by machines compared to 46% today.
Therefore, these high technological skillful job change will bring negative influence to some demotive-skillful or low skillful labors to be dismissed, if they can not upgrade or raise or reskillgul their skill level to improve their analytical thinking , technology design and programming skills to cooperate with (AI) tools to work efficiently together in any organizational manufacturing or offie work environment. Because it will have many employers apply (AI) automation tools to participate with blue -color or whiate -color workers' tasks in order to raise efficiencies or improve performance in any working environment. So, it is right time to young or mid age employees need to upskill and/or reskill their rihgt type of skills to prepare future technology risch work environment changeing needs.
Future technological advances will permit an increasing number of tasks traditionally performed by humans to become automated. It seems that , such automation focused primarily on routine tasks, e.g. clerical work, bookkeeping, basic paralegal work and reporting etc. However, with the advent of big data, artificial intelligence (AI), the internet of things and ever-increasing computing power , i.e. the digital revolutions, non-routine tasks are also increasingly likely to become automated. For example, the recent development in robotics and 3D printing allow firms in advanced economies to locate production closer to domestic markets in fully aumomated factories. As a result, the future strongest incentive to automate because of their relatively

higher labour costs will be reduced, when production automated will bring the negative influence to dismiss some foolish or low produtive or low skill workers , the owning high automated productive skillful workers will replace the low productive skillful workers in any factories' manufacturing environments. So, technological progress participates to raise quantity of jobs will cause result in significant job losses to low skillful workers. Because future employers will need many high automated productive employees to help them to cooperate with (AI) automated machine to work together efficiently. For example, many proportion of occupations at high risk is greatest in Germany and lowest in Korea, these countries organizations will accept to spend technology investments and education of workers to prepare future automatability manufacturing development successfully.

However, future automatability manufacturing development will bring technological unemployment in possible, due to workers need to adjust to the challenge of automation by switching tasks. Thus, preventing technological unemployment, also technological change does not just destroy jobs, but also generates new roles through its effect on productivity and the demand for new technologies. For example, it has been estimated that, for each high tech-job created in the industries , such as computing equipment or electrical machinery, some 4.9 % additional jobs are created for lawyers, taxi, drivers and waites in the local economy (Moretti, 2011).

Therefore, automated will also influence service industries' job nature change, e.g. taxi drivers need to apply (AI) automated machines to assist them to drive their taxis. When the passenger tells the taxi driver where he/she wants to go. Then, the (AI automated machine will follow the GPS road direction map to be indicated how to drive the taxi to go to the destination automatically . So, future taxi driver is one assistance role to assist the (AI) automated driving tool to dominate the (AI) tool to drive the taxi to catch the passenger to arrive the destination safety in the short time in possible. For another example, future restaurant waiters will need (AI) automated machines's assistance to help them to deliver or dispatch any foods and soft drinks to send to the identified eater's table carefully in accurate and efficient service performance way from the kitchen, in especially in the busy time and many people are sitting in the large size restaurant environment. So, future, waiter roles will be the leader , they need to manage or control or supervise the (AI) robotics how to make decisions to arrange to dispatch which foods or soft drinks to the different tables in preference immediately. Also, future law clerks need to supervise or manage the law robotics how to help them to make decisions to do revision or draft or filing legal tasks in preference in order to avoid any typing words are mistaken to type on computers or revised draft in wrong way to assist manual legal clerks' mistaken words are appearanced on any legal documents. So, the law clerk future role will be the trainer role , he/she eeds to teacher the robots how to check any words, e.g. grammers to correct them to be right grammers, or giving the accurate revision legal documents' instruction to let the legal robots to know how to revise each legal draft to prove whether which part of the legal draft will have wrong to be needed to revise.

In conclusion, future many manual workers' service or manfacturing job natures will become automated assistance to robotics. So, employees need to upgrade their skills in order to adopt new technological work nature change. So future CEO needs to prepare to learn how to apply robotic technological skills to train workers to raise efficiencies and improve performance because there are many future organizations start to apply robotic manufacturing tools to assist workers to work in any departments. Hence, future excellent CEOs must need to own AI knowledge to satisfy their organizational performance improvement need.

9 798886 840056

Printed by Libri Plureos GmbH in Hamburg, Germany